Anna Barker

Book of Crow

Indigo Dreams Publishing

First Edition: Book of Crow
First published in Great Britain in 2023 by:
Indigo Dreams Publishing
24, Forest Houses
Cookworthy Moor
Halwill
Beaworthy
Devon
EX21 5UU

www.indigodreamspublishing.com

ISBN 978-1-912876-79-2

British Library Cataloguing in Publication Data. A CIP record for this book can be obtained from the British Library.

Designed and typeset in Palatino Linotype by Indigo Dreams.
Cover Art by Ronnie Goodyer ©Ronnie Goodyer 2023
Author photo by Paul Crowther www.revolverphoto.com
Interior illustrations by Sean Collins.
Printed and bound in Great Britain by 4edge Ltd.

Papers used by Indigo Dreams are recyclable products made from wood grown in sustainable forests following the guidance of the Forest Stewardship Council.

for Ben

Acknowledgements

Acknowledgements are due to the editors of the following publications where some of these poems, or earlier versions of them, first appeared:
Acumen, The Interpreter's House, Tabula Rasa (Linen Press, 2023), Speaking Stones (North Pens, 2023), Typehouse Literary Magazine.

I would like to thank Valentina Erastova for her encyclopaedic knowledge of corvids, and her rescue crow, Hamlet, for his mischief. Thanks, too, to jackdaws, Ozzy and Beatle, who trained their human well.

I would like to thank Clare Shaw for their diligence and faith during the polishing of this manuscript and for their generosity, humour and friendship. Thanks also to the Wonky Animals Poetry Collective for their welcome and warmth and to my True North pals: Marina, Tina, and Heather for their feedback and encouragement.

Lastly, gratitude to Ronnie and Dawn, for welcoming Crow into the Indigo Dreams family and to Pat, David and Jessie, for their unending love and support.

Book of Crow

Call me Crow,
your feathered Almighty,
hallowed be my name.
Thy will be done as I tell it.

Crow is sulking
the rain-heavy wing
the ruinous prophecy

Crow is the black tongue
the tap of conscience
the shadow passing

Crow is the deep incision
the twisted root
the souls turned out of their bodies

Crow is the rib of winter
the trees bending to speak to themselves
the easing back of form

Crow is the last word.

Let me tell you how fucking insane I am,
let me tell you about that night
how, as Mum swung from her neck,

I sat alone in the dark.
Let me tell you what I did.
I drank that sweet, black milk,

I let black run in me,
find a home in me
as it'd found a home in her.

Black nests now in my belly –
she's still here because of it,
like the lullaby she hummed

when she forgot the words.
Let me tell you how sometimes
black is a crow

big and proud and gleaming,
how I know he isn't real but
let me tell you how fucking insane I am:

I see him clear as I see you.

Ah! My reflection in a glass –
a god with feathers!
Tink, tink, pleased to meet me,
no time to chat, there's work to do.

Empty bottle, cork top, stinking sock,
radiator HOT,
pack-gakka-plop.
Shiny taps, bathroom snacks
of soap and floss.

Oops, your lips are moving:
things you forgot to say?
Where do you go when you sleep?
Back to her?

I'm home, I whisper, and your eyes flutter.
I lift the duvet, poke my head in:
a fug of sweat, nipples, a spider's nest.
For hours I sit on your chest,
rising and falling in time with your breath

until at last, you heave yourself up,
lumber and slump onto the toilet to piss.

Your pain. Your sagging breasts.
Your questions.

Back to bed, funny feathers.

I see her when I close my eyes,
her high brow, doll-heavy lids,
her hand, curled,
as though the sum of me
might fit into her palm.

My child's eye made no sense of it
amazed only by how
tall she'd grown in the night.
Then I understood.

Feet dangling,
belt at her neck
the great orbiting planet of her head,
and oh my god

the shock
of her beautiful, beautiful body.
Give me instead

the kicked-away bedroom chair,
the bin bags stuffed with her clothes,
the salty tang of sandals in Tesco bags.

Do you remember *Kerplunk!*?
You lift your eyes from the book you're failing to read.
Or the marbles I thought were fisheyes?
You brush a money spider from the page.

Or your Dad, who washed your hair
with the cherry shampoo that
smelled of your Mum.
Smelled of her skin, skin, skin...

Sentimental? I eat baby rabbits!
I'll fetch you one if you doubt it.
I'm a murderous hawker of darkness,
carcass-eating, death-dealing, soul-taking priest of sorrow.

Oh, be quiet, Crow.

I remember when you zipped
across the lawn bearing gifts:
bottle tops, cake crumbs, bacon fat.

A peculiar sight. Barefoot,
disher-dashing, breath clouds
parping the air.

You spoke in chitter-chats,
wonderful sounds that
spiralled up to my high perch.

A sign of happiness?
Happy like a rabbit
when it can't see

the gun.

Where's this – Tynemouth? In the photograph
there's a heft of cloud. A day to make the best of it
she might've said.

Dad took it, maybe he weighed up
who to put in the frame;
Mum at the water's edge, eyes lowered, looking.

At her feet, I suppose.
I try on the view, see her long toes,
ghosts in the amber kelp

and the razor shell she could've chosen for me.
What would I be? Six, maybe seven.
Not old enough to feel the cold.

Digging a channel, shouting
until at last she saw me –

briefly.

The holiday cottage in Guernsey
had a goose who guarded the outside loo.
We were supposed to go in twos
but Lorna pissed in a bucket instead.

Dad studied the map,
drew lines in pencil
to places that grew tomatoes.
Tomatoes are big in Guernsey, he said.

The storm brought us together.
Weather worth watching
our three breaths clouding the glass
while outside
the wind carried the goose up and up.

When it was over we went outside,
us three
and were amazed to see owls
on fence posts, owls on stone walls,
owls on park benches.

They look pissed, Lorna said.

It's shock, said Dad.

Only I knew it was grief.

I enter the room on a draught,
find you on the bed.

You snort,
release a long breath:

dead shrew, notes of Jim Beam.
Slug tongue.

Tug it, toss it,
Don't peck!

Hither and thither,
head down, skitter.

A kiss
for the child I remember.

The counsellor has an Aztec blue sofa
with a yellow felt-tip stain
she hides with a cushion.

She wants to talk about attachment,
I want to talk about the stain.
I'm afraid that's my daughter's doing –

Grace, sometimes Gracie, she's eight.
Nearly nine.
Funny, how she tags on that last line –

an invitation, perhaps
to talk about my childhood.
Hell of a leap, mind: from *nine*

to Mum's suicide,
but I've given her bugger-all to work with.
Sixty-five quid an hour for this shit.

She's got me pegged
already I'll bet – depression, anxiety.
PTSD with a question mark.

What *was* I like as a child?
Fucked if I know.
Tell her something, though, anything,

describe a drawing with a yellow sun,
me and Mum on the swings,
crows closing in.

When I was nine years old
I dug up the neighbour's cat
to feel the weight of her bones

in my hands. It took longer
than I expected but I worked with the
patience of a gardener

or one who knew the importance
of exposing a fraud.
With the earth piled by my thighs,

I lifted her from the grave,
cradled her fur and bone,
light as a feather in my lap.

Sheba. I spoke her name aloud.
Sheba. Who sunbathed in rose bushes
all summer, Sheba

who chattered at the pigeons,
who clearly, now that I saw her,
was not sleeping.

Gently, I carried her
to her new grave –
a pillow of moss

encircled with daisy heads
and dandelion clocks
so all would see their lie.

you told me to up my mettle
not to settle for what

those marzipan girls
with their Babyliss curls said

about my tits – so what
if they're cherry pips?

they're full of shit, you said,
they lie about the dicks they've had

all they got is Jason Donovan
wet dreams running downstream.

You said forgetting would make me clean
that the past would become a blank screen

if I followed you into the dark
if I followed you into the dark.

There's craft to this depression,
akin to making God's Eyes.
Patience, technique.

I find it helps to think in catchphrases,
inspirational live-bys
to stick on the fridge. A few here from you, I see,
in your crowly scrawl –

Dance. Be the storm.

You are not the brick. You are the wall.

Reach for the moon. Fall.

I try to talk about Mum but he says
bones and dust, bones and dust
and it's all the same to him.

So I lock myself in the bathroom
where once he found me.
Does he even remember?

We drank from the tap,
vowels rising like moons in his beak.
I hear him now, trying to get in,

scratting at the door like a rat.
For God's sake!
Silence then,

the drip-clunk of the tap.
I didn't mean it. Come back!
I burst onto the landing,

run from room to room,
find feathers long and black,
race downstairs, mislay my legs,

take flight, hit the tiles
with a crack.
Black.

Sound. Scuffles, scratches,
oily warm breath.
Turning my head,

I see he's offered me
feathers, dead leaves –
a nest.

Grief doesn't have *six* stages:
'denial, anger, bargaining…
something, blah, blah, something…'

It's like that time you read the Bible,
<u>He</u> said *death would be no more,*
promised an end to your mourning,

and here you are, still hurting.
Forget salvation,
faith is for rabbits caught in the beam.

Grief is bitter as coal,
strong as wild garlic,
rank as meat left out for a week,

baby robins plundered from the nest,
voodoo threats, blood sport,
rancour, eating the eyes first,

the watch on your wrist,
ticking, years and years
after she

stopped.

Last night I dreamt I grew wings
of blackish blue. I shone, almost,

so alive, so bone light
I flew.

When at last I perched,
I spoke nonsense words

only I could understand:
clacks and clicks,

sharp sounds
that fell from my beak

like ink.
Then, stretching my wings,

I saw a time
so sublime it seemed invented:

gloves stitched to string,
Monopoly Tuesdays,

Maggie, the cat,
spooled in a basket.

You stole my grief,
the attention.
That's what she said.
My big sister calls me a thief.

Like there's not enough of
this shit to go around,
like that time I stole
the pink crown from

Mum's birthday cake and
Lorna called me a cunt.
That word.
Dad slamming his fist so hard

ice cubes leapt from
my Coke like salmon.
Did Mum even notice?
Her face was mist.

While we fought
over who'd committed
the bigger crime,
was she remaking us

from pink paper napkins,
hand-locked,
paper-doll chain sisters
cut from her own image?

Into the growing ache of this home I bring
the leaf,
the snail in his shell,
the silver hair on a bud.

You don't want them.

So I give you the unfolding season,
the cage of the dandelion clock,
the quick water of a stream,
the cold breath of a shadow.

You don't want them.

So I give you the muteness of mud,
the tossed egg,
the dry mouth of a cave,
the hard news of a pilfered nest.

The cows, a scrum,
shoulder to shoulder, formed a ring,
rapt by Dad's rendition of the Beatles.

And Mum, she was
a bright halo, hair scraped back,
sunburned neck. Laughing.

I want to hold it –
that laugh,
though it's not like

the field mazed with pats,
the stonewall we struggled to climb,
the sandwiches she remembered to pack

could ever excuse her last
heavy
fall.

He was singing Strawberry Fields,
that's it, and she was laughing
the way people do when something's

both funny and tragic.
But the cows didn't hurt him.
They weren't even unfriendly.

Just one, perhaps,
swaying forward, as though
to test her courage.

The matriarch, darker than the rest.

You leave slugs on my pillow
to get me out of bed. You peck an apple
so I'll have to eat the rest.

You tell me you're hunting spiders when
really you're dissecting my
hope-to-get-fucked knickers.

You call this behaviour 'intervention'
a get-out-of-bed, out-of-my-own-head
breakdown cessation.

Fine, we can sit here among the snowdrops
in the weak spring sun. I'll smoke cigarettes;
we'll call it fun.

Get a job? You sound like my sister:
socks up, glass down
but you don't know what it's like,

drinking all day, raging all night
I mightn't even be
depressed – sometimes I laugh.

I don't drink because I have a problem,
I drink because the world is
a problem – I drink to fit.

We slide together
my flesh, your feather.

Your jet eye, the haw you draw across in sleep.
The patient keel of your sternum –
the steel of your rib.

Your beak to stitch the vane, the silken ley,
the tap of talons on glass,
the hollow bone that lends my shape.

Your pulse of blood – smell of hot metal –
stash in the kettle.
The word you hold in your throat like an egg.

You're asleep on my wool scarf,
fluffed up.
If I look at you long enough
you change shape,
into a monster
then into a mother,
in a blink,

Crow again.

Breath not bottle.
This bottle? Tink-tink*!*
Breath not boTtle.
You're not drinking.
Breath not bottle.
Oh, I see   it's that game
Breath   not   bottle
       the one called trying not to drink
breath nob bottle
     I love games
breath shutthefuckup bottle
       I could play   devil's advocate
    beffs not bevils
   drink   and you'll get the taste for it
   BREATH   NO   BOTTLE
drink   you're bound to get wasted

   breath botbottlenot

drink

BREA

drink   by ten 'o'clock you'll be texting your exes

breaTHnOt ^o-b-8

drink   and you'll be begging for *cock*

CROW!

I wish you could see yourself
trying on that laugh,
prinking and preening

like a popinjay.
Does your lover know
you only do the rump-garruffing,

pot the hole, sloppy-mot,
fleabagging
just to feel something

when nothing is too much?
Pour yourself another drink!
Your pheromones are making me sick.

I'll go sit outside in the rain.

I find you passed out,
bottle of whiskey, no glass,
pissy jeans,

four surprising flavours of vomit.
From your mouth
a delicious spider-thread of drool.

What about me? Do I not amaze
when I murder
the dawn chorus?

Wake up, I'm bored.
I need conversation,
it took years to learn words

and your self-pity
hinders my evolution.
Wake up, funny feathers,

pay me some attention,
this could still work,
you and me.

Take this rabbit,
or more precisely its parts.

See here the spleen, the intestine,
the kidneys, the heart,
the sheen of the iliocostalis,
the sweet cherry gush of the aortic arch.

The oesophagus: always tough.
The pancreatic duct,
the half-digested stink in the tranverse duodenum,
the cecum appendix.

How glorious she is,
this language –
this meat.

Happy birthday to me,
happy birthday to me. Do you see
what I've become?

Let me cut you a slice
of bone-dry sarcasm.
A sliver of rage? Just for the taste.

My grief is a mouthful,
claggy at the edges,
take a wodge of blind panic instead.

Candles? Thirty, of course.
A flame for every wasted year,
a flame for every tail chased,

every bad choice.
Gather round, raise your glass,
the toast is near.

napkin toss napkin toss napkin toss   lentil leaf wrap
crap   fuck off
      this   chicken curry dressed up   TIKKAKAKA
parsnip crisp?
       meh
    peck
toss
        peck
toss
blubbie pop   KAVIAR JACKPOP gakkaktastic POP POP!
uh
     tittybittles gone   where's the pretty pretty pilchard then
eh   eh?   fish eye?
peck
     toss   toss   whats   *this*?   butternutmush
NOT A NUT! ATTACK!!
peck   toss   ooooh   crabs on puffy cracks!
stash stash stash
wild mushroom   not wild
          BIRTHDAY CAAAAAKE!
this? fuck worm? SAUSAGE tug-gak-gak-tug-gak-gak
       egg   no chick   no point
             pancetta, uppity
      salmon, ug-ug-ug
(plastic plastic plastic   fork)
       ahaaaak! Prize PORK PIE bottomatthebottom
       FATgoo goo j'oob

halfway to rot

Yes, I pecked.
Of course I did.

I popped the blue fat on her ankles,
I tore at the flesh between her ribs

I left her eyes though.
I left her eyes.

Other crows would not have been
so kind.

It's this sort of misunderstanding
that makes the food chain so frustrating.

I am, of course, of my own making,
I go back longer than your dead mother swinging:

you see this foot? Millions of years of evolution,
I outlived Darwin and I'm still evolving.

I stash roadkill in your toaster,
I shit on your fuck-me knickers,

I have the ear of the Boris,
I am a murderer of baby rabbits.

How much more real could I be?

I won't think about him,
not tonight. Not after our fight.
I just want this pill,

a blue-vein thrill to
pad out the party vibe
until I'm sliding

into the organ-warmth,
a beautiful shimmering slipstream,
a back-of-the-throat beat scene that makes me

dance.
Dance,

split myself on a beam of light,
unspool and bloom,
take flight.

frozen crackles and stars   steam
    rising
  from
vents
the day of reckonings come n the ayes have it the ayes have it

                                     up there

  CROW that you
                       bloody pigeons

for shes a jolly good fellow   are you getting this

         shit itss and giggles or kicks isit   forgotten   lost me
song

where you at

CROW

                       you'll be about somewhere   a form a
                  shape a dark breath all my own blah   blah
  CROW
        nope
          not under
              the bridge
maybes   across the street

dont beeps your horn at me   hey watchit

iloveyouiloveyouiloveyou
        not you   thoughts you was someone
        CROW

eh what dysay saythatagain wanna see my TiTs

Someone get her a taxi.

too bloody right busses s shite   bring me bottle tops   shiny
scraps   im here

          CROW
rotting squirrel if you please s not fussy swigsit   sickit
swigsomemore...
                    where the bloody hell am I   statue
monsument   no   a   grave
               moons dropped itself ina puddsel look
                              light there party im coming
          peoplepartywheredtheygo   that way
          no
   this way
nope
lost my way
lost I'm snot lost   dont   tell   me   what   I   am

shadows fattening

crow. take me home

In the house while you're out,
I'm hard at work.

I pull the wool from your scarf.
I shit on the wires at the back of the telly.
I stash my feathers in places you'll not find
for years and years.

One day I'll be gone
and you'll miss me.

I don't know how long you've been gone,
days, weeks, years.
Is this what it's like to miss someone –

here, alone in a tree,
a dog shit bag impersonating me?
Wood lice, look.

When you were little
you called them chuggy-pigs.
Love is unbecoming of me.

All time runs through me,
the water and the wind. And yet ...
the way your top lip

hangs over your bottom lip
when you sleep.
Night falls.

People, rolling bottles, clip-clop heels,
drunken laughter.
I shout for you from a frosty perch,

your name
so stretched and thin it
frightens me.

My dead Mum hanging by her neck
is beautiful,
bent like a new fern,
feet pointed in a way a ballerina might envy,
her hands half-way to a gesture.

It holds me, her shape.
Had she stayed, we'd have shared our love of it,
how it goes on and on.
My dead Mum hanging by her neck
is beautiful.

You've been avoiding me.
I understand,
giving up the booze was bound
to provoke synaptic misfiring.
How long is it now?
Are we still counting in hours?

Whatever gets you through.
I'm fine.
I'm filing
your childhood
in alphabetical order:

acorns, anemones, art,
aerobics, anxiety,
arson (algebra), aerosol deodorant,
amazing grace (recorder),
blood blister, burping (alphabet),
Barbie massacre,
burial,

crow, crow, crow....

White.
White sheets, white knuckles,
white pearls I spit out and stash in white pillows.

You perch at the foot of my bed,
a pulp of black feathers,
sick with what you've swallowed.

The nurses say the words scored on my wrists are not yours,
they say you are not a god with feathers,
they say you are a pain I can choose to leave.

I will not.
I will plumb the darkness for you,
I will not be the other me,

the unwanted guest who sits by this bed,
who is neither ugly nor beautiful,
neither sick nor well.

You open your beak, a wordless cry,
unfold your wing,
lay it over me like a wreath.

At visiting hour you return,
invite yourself in,
hang yourself up on the chair.

You are quiet,
warmed in gilded light,
feathers puffed like a sail.

More pelt than feather,
you gleam, like an otter,
preen with the relish of a cat.

I cannot bear to grieve
the cleft of your wing,
your diamond and coal,

the caul of your third lid.

You still live.
I'll bring you in from the cold.

Hold you close.
How familiar you are.

Sorry
for thinking I could move on.

I'm done

trying to do this alone.
Come,

find your place inside me,
know you are home.

Shock clags the back of the throat –
a cough releases the stink
of rotting mouse.

Loss must be chased like wind.
When caught, it smells of
newly-birthed rabbits.

Sadness trudges. A decisive
stomp of the foot is enough to snare it.
Its smell is cheese left out to sweat.

And me? What do I smell of?
I breathe from the cavern of your ear. Hope.
Today you smell of hope.

I'm hacking at the daffodils in the garden
with a blunt kitchen knife.

Let's have them inside, I say
no good out here

cheering everyone else up.
You say happiness is foolish,

that Thalia's mask will never fit
a face so comfortable with grief.

What will I recall of this
cool, spring afternoon?

The smashed vase,
or your attempt at love?

I dreamt I was an eel
in the moon-wet blaze of a river,
one of dozens bellied in the reeds,
slack-mouthed, slick as liver.

At the summon of the moon,
I bloomed onto land,
a singular, taut muscle,
flexing through the cool lick of grass.

I was bones in a trough,
the silver knot on a tree,
old leaves read as braille,
the moon's ribs on the beach.

I was the way,
the hoar trail
up the slip of the bank, down
the gallows drop to the lane.

To be a King
you must commit to flesh, not waste it,
revere darkness as the crucible from which all life is made.
Fear children, they are unpredictable, tasteless.
Accept you are easily distracted,
but never put your back to danger.
Be heard, when a King speaks he should bellow,
or not bother.
Never trust snow or good intentions,
or people who leave the lights on.
Show doubters your tail feathers,
play each one like a chord against the light.
Practice rituals of your own invention,
lest it messes with the natural order.
Accept that to love is to be conflicted,
never to know what to do for the best.

Fear the snake.

I watch you ransack a rabbit, though it's not 'til you flip it
I see the scut.
You show me the easy-in, an incision wide enough to bury your head
then up and up
under a skirt of skin to unhitch the lumbar vertebrae.

There's tenderness in your work, or precision. I pretend to
know the difference
while on a stone you lay the bags and pipes, find an end;
show me
the heart, the stomach, the spleen.

Looking at you, I see a surgeon, or an artist or
something in-between,
not the violence that frightened me so much I hid
until you'd preened
yourself clean.

Feel the old bones
on their way to ash, the cat shit,
the blind worm.

The pull of roots, the lost marble,
the inert bulbs whispering
what they could've been.

The hold of clay.
The rotting mulch
still warm with the life

of the flower,
the leaf.
Green shoots.

Not inconceivable
something could grow
from all this.

That I might one day
stand up,
wipe my hands clean.

Know better the ease of things.

Crows are suspicious of snow,
its conspiracy with the moon,
its dulling of crowness.
Piss potholes, slim pickings.

Just a flurry, don't fuss,
winter's last gripe, that's all.
You scoop it into your hands,
bring it inside.

Have you gone mad?
Snow isn't to keep, but you
laugh and make a game of dotting it
on the end of my beak.

I flatten like a cat,
flay and spit.
You laugh some more.
To hear you laugh like that

is good, I think.

You sit like tar poured and set.

I sometimes forget how old you are –
you're handsome, even beautiful,
but what of your time-worried eye?

How does it end for a god with feathers?
I couldn't bear to see you dead.
I won't say goodbye.

However this ends, it can't end with grief.

I shall make Crow a nest.
I'll take my time with it,
make it nice, line it with pages from *The Spectator*.

Now and then, I'll sit with him,
we'll chat about the weather.
Sometimes he'll pass comment on
the sticky demise of *the Boris*.

Occasionally, I'll bring him gifts,
nothing too fancy, small things:
sea glass from my walks at the beach.
Something that reminds him

there are things he doesn't know.
In Spring, I'll fetch him a cut of lamb,
we'll listen to the sap rising.

There'll be times, I'm sure,
when I'll not visit him for weeks,
years, though I know I'll miss him.

Of course I'll miss him.

Fuck off, Florence
I don't need a nightingale!

Visit me? You should be so lucky
I will be too busy ruling

the kingdoms of my making.
I have ambitions

far greater than anything
you could muster.

No, thank you.
I'm thrilled you're embracing the light

it's about time you started
flapping those wings

but let's be honest –
though we had a good thing going

I was getting bored
listening to your shit.

Rabbit,

glanced by a car, paralysed,
but not dead.

Konk, I pop its marble eye
as a voice from the hedge whispers
corvidae ad infinitum.

Dance, dance,
trip on the furry stink,
peck, hammer,   crack,
ah, there we are,

we're in,
splash, squirt, rip, snip,
oops, too much,
vomit it back,   splash

in the eye,
blinded,
blink, blink,
stand tall, who's that?
Aaak! It's
mine,
mine.

And when I'm done I'm done,
mired in filth, mop top,
scarved in guts
eyes of malice,
eyes of loathing.

Corvidae ad infinitum.

Indigo Dreams Publishing Ltd
24, Forest Houses
Cookworthy Moor
Halwill
Beaworthy
Devon
EX21 5UU
www.indigodreamspublishing.com